In memory of the fallen from Bampton.

With thanks to the Year 5 & 6 children at Bampton Primary School (2024/25) for their help with this project.

FIRST PUBLISHED 2025
CITYSCAPE PUBLISHING
ISBN: 978-1-9164164-9-9

TEXT COPYRIGHT © ANDREW POWELL-THOMAS, 2025

THE MORAL RIGHT OF THE AUTHOR HAS BEEN ASSERTED UNDER THE COPYRIGHT, DESIGNS AND PATENTS ACT, 1988. A CIP CATALOGUE RECORD FOR THIS BOOK IS AVAILABLE FROM THE BRITISH LIBRARY.

ALL RIGHTS RESERVED

THE CONTENTS OF THIS BOOK ARE BELIEVED CORRECT AT THE TIME OF PRINTING. NEVERTHELESS, THE PUBLISHERS CANNOT BE HELD RESPONSIBLE FOR ANY ERRORS OR OMISSIONS IN THE DETAILS GIVEN IN THIS BOOK.

FRONT COVER CLOCKWISE FROM TOP LEFT: F.J. CANDLER; BAMPTON WAR MEMORIAL; S.J. JONES; GRAVE OF WILLIAM PARSONS (TYNE COT CEMETERY).
BACK COVER: BAMPTON WAR MEMORIAL.

BAMPTON REMEMBERS

ANDREW POWELL-THOMAS

ISBN: 978-1-9164164-9-9

CONTENTS

- 6   Remembering the fallen
- 9   St Michael & All Angels Church

10	Harry Attwater	42	Edmund Hancock
12	Walter Batstone	44	Frederick Hutchings
13	Fred Bowden	46	Alfred Hutter
14	Francis Brice	48	Arthur Kerslake
16	Charles Budd	49	Horace Kingdom
18	Herbert Burnett	50	Richard Lugg
20	John Burton	52	Tom Mantle
21	Thomas Burnett	53	Gilbert Nott
22	Francis Candler	54	Sydney Parsons
24	William Cottrell	56	William Parsons
26	Charles Curtis	58	Frederick Rabjohns
27	Arthur Davey	60	Ernest Serenger
28	A Dunster	62	Sydney Stevens
29	William Escott	64	Felix Tarr
30	James Gage	66	Isaac Thorne
32	W Gardener	68	Frank Tooze
34	Michael Gibbings	70	Henry Tucker
36	William Gibbings	71	Thomas Vickery
37	Arthur Gillard	72	Frederick Ware
38	John Greenslade	74	Charley Toze
39	Reginald Greenslade	75	Anketell Moutray Read VC
40	William Greenslade	78	Hugh Acland Troyte
80	Stanley Alderman	90	Sydney Jones
82	Victor Brown	92	P Hutchings
84	Kenneth Burnett	93	Edward Kennard
85	Felix Cottrell	94	William Mogridge
86	Gilbert Cottrell	96	J Partridge
88	G Evans	97	Frederick Woodman
89	Reginald Floyde		

- 98   Remembrance
- 99   Acknowledgments

REMEMBERING THE FALLEN

In the years that followed the First World War, the biggest ever wave of public commemoration saw tens of thousands of memorials erected right across the commonwealth, and the town of Bampton in Devon was no different. Numerous men had left their quiet life in the country to fight on battlefields right across the world, from the trenches of Flanders to the deserts in the Middle East, with some never to return.

The joy and celebration of Armistice in 1918 was understandably darkened for many with the sense of loss they had suffered - the parish had lost 'some of their own' and everyone knew someone who had grieved.

Memorials to the fallen were designed and created as a necessary act of remembrance right across the country, but constructing them was often a fraught process. Parish councils had little money themselves to go towards building them, and they relied on donations and fundraising from the local community to raise the necessary amount. It is not surprising that those who had lost loved ones felt more of a burden to contribute, and if a community was fortunate, a wealthy local benefactor may have been able to provide significant backing to the building costs.

Opinions often differed as to the best form and location for a war memorial and there is no reason to believe the community of Bampton was any different - keeping everyone appeased was a delicate process.

A granite cross on a three-stepped base, with a wall and railings behind and fronted by metal posts and chains, was positioned at the junction of High Street and the South Molton Road. It was unveiled in October 1921 by W.C. Carnell, a blinded war veteran, J. Penwarden J.P. and the Rev. E.V. Cox.

Forty-one men from the parish lost their lives during the First World War, with their names inscribed on three sides.

  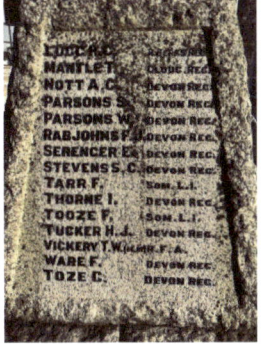

A little over twenty years later the Second World War began, and the thirteen names of those lost from the area were added on the top step of the memorial, along with a small marker at the front for one of these men, laid on behalf of Bampton Home Guard.

In 2015, a commemorative slab was placed at the foot of the memorial to mark the service of Captain Anketell Moutray Read VC, and an additional name was added to the memorial.

Today, they stand as a testament to the bravery of those who paid the ultimate price in the fight for freedom that we take for granted today. Lest we forget.

ST MICHAEL AND ALL ANGELS CHURCH

A plaque was also placed in the town's church, along with the glass of a beautiful stained glass window being replaced in the memory of the fallen men. An additional plaque was added after the Second World War.

HARRY ATTWATER

Service Number: 675457
Rank: Private
    38th Battalion
    Canadian Infantry
Born: 1890
Died: 14 April 1918
Buried: Roclincourt Military Cemetery, France

Harry Falconer Attwater was born in 1890 to Henry and Eliza Attwater, who at that time were living in Brittain Street. The outbreak of the Great War provided many men with an opportunity to earn steady money, as well providing them with a sense of adventure, and Harry signed up to the 38th Battalion of the Canadian Infantry - the Eastern Ontario Regiment, when they arrived in England in June 1916.

Sailing across the English Channel in mid-August, they were thrust into the Western Front, with the battalion seeing action at Grandcourt and Vimy Ridge. They spent the winter of 1917/1918 in the Avion area and held various sections between the towns of *Oppy* and *Loos*. It was whilst here, in the vicinity of *Hill 70*, that Harry lost his life on 14 April 1918.

His parents received news of his death on 23 April 1918, *St George's Day*, in a letter from the Lieutenant of the platoon. Dated 17 April, it explained that Harry was killed instantly by a heavy shell whilst holding a post on the front line with four other men.

Harry Attwater is buried in plot IV. C. 2. at Roclincourt Military Cemetery. Roclincourt is a small village in the Pas de Calais region of northern France between Arras and Lens, and the cemetery was first opened in April 1917.

Today it contains 916 commonwealth graves, 32 of which are sadly unidentified, along with 4 German burials. Many of the burials here are from the first few days of fighting of the Battle of Arras.

Roclincourt Military Cemetery, France

WALTER BATSTONE

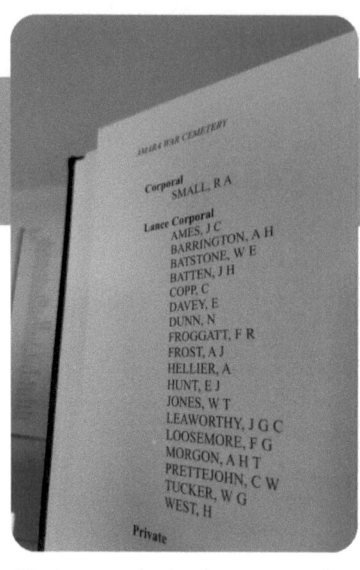

Service Number: 200105
Rank: Lance Corporal
   1st/4th Devonshire Regiment
Born: Unknown
Died: 24 July 1917
Buried: Amara War Cemetery, Iraq

Not much is known about Walter Edmund Batstone, whose name also features on the nearby Huntsham village War Memorial. He enlisted with the 4th Devonshire Regiment who went to India and Mesopotamia (Iraq). After being involved in the significant attack on the *Hai Salient*, they were mainly occupied with building roads and establishing the *Tigris* defences and lines of communication.

Walter died, likely from illness, on 24 July 1917 and was buried in plot XIV. A. 1. at Amara War Cemetery. Over 4500 men are buried here, but in the 1930s all the headstones were removed due to salt in the soil causing them to deteriorate. Their names were then engraved on a large screen wall, as well as being recorded in a Roll of Honour at the Commonwealth War Grave Commission's Head Office.

FRED BOWDEN

Service Number: 865508
Rank: Private
    52nd Battalion
    Canadian Regiment
Born: 1882
Died: 29 December 1917
Commemorated: Loos British Cemetery, France

Fred Bowden was born to Alfred and Barbara Bowden of Bampton. He married Jane and they lived at 1 Newport Street, Tiverton before he enlisted with the 52nd Battalion of the Canadian Infantry. He was sadly killed on 29 December 1917 and is commemorated on panel 29 at the Loos British Cemetery.

FRANCIS BRICE

Service Number: K/22007
Rank: Stoker First Class
HMS Candytuft
Born: 1894
Died: 18 November 1917
Commemorated:
Plymouth Naval Memorial

Born in 1894, Francis James Brice was born to Samuel and Bessie Brice of Dayles Cottage in nearby Petton.

The outbreak of the First World War saw him join the Royal Navy. As a stoker, he was one of many men responsible for feeding coal to the boilers and he became one of the 97 crew of *HMS Candytuft*, an escort sloop launched in May 1917.

HMS Candytuft was a Q-ship, deliberately designed to look like a merchant vessel but having hidden weapons. The idea was that enemy U-boats would move into vulnerable attacking positions thinking this was an undefended vessel, before the hidden weapons would strike the submarine.

On 18 November 1917 it was escorting the merchant vessel *SS Tremayne* from Gibraltar to Malta, when they came under attack from *U-39*. A torpedo blew off the stern and it is likely that this was the moment that Francis Brice, along with a number of others, lost their lives. The order was given to abandon ship, whilst secretly keeping the gun crews on board to man their hidden weapons, hoping the submarine would surface. It didn't and the guns fired at its periscope, leading to the U-boat to fire a second torpedo at its bow.

With the boat torn in two, the bow section sank almost immediately, whilst the remainder of wreck drifted before grounding near *Cape Bigli*.

The boats two 4-inch guns were the only things salvageable and the survivors were picked up by a French trawler.

Francis James Brice is commemorated on panel 22 of the large Plymouth Naval Memorial, along with 23000 others lost at sea and who have no known grave.

CHARLES BUDD

Service Number: 187527
Rank: Private
8th Battalion
Canadian Regiment
Born: 1895
Died: 15 August 1917
Commemorated: Vimy Memorial, France

Born in Stoodleigh in 1895 to George and Sarah Budd, by the outbreak of the First World War the family were living at Three Corners Farm, Cove - just on the outskirts of Bampton.

Charles joined the 8th Battalion of the Canadian Regiment when they arrived in Britain in the autumn of 1914. In 1915 they left for the western front, and they remained there for the duration of the conflict. Nicknamed *'The Little Black Devils of Canada'*, they participated in a number of the most well-known battles of the Great War, including the Somme, Vimy and Passchendaele - and it was during this battle that Charles Budd lost his life on 15 August 1917.

As well as remembering the fallen, the Vimy Memorial also has a number of Great War trench lines, and battlefield terrain, preserved in a natural state.

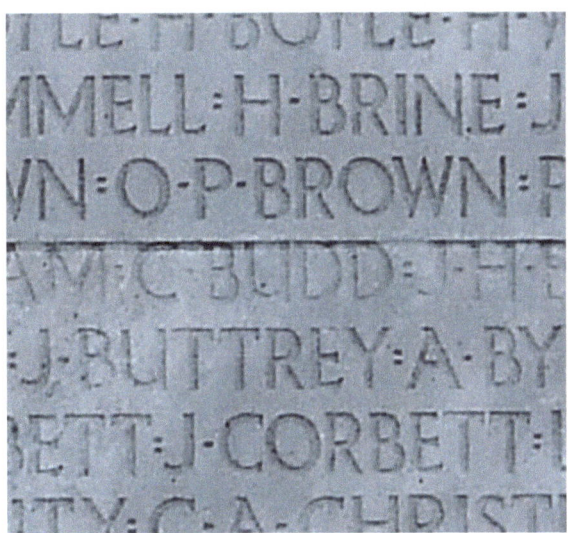

Charles Budd's name is commemorated on on the Vimy Memorial - a 250 acre site dedicated to the memory of Canadian soldiers who lost their life during the conflict. There are 11,000 names here of men who have no known grave.

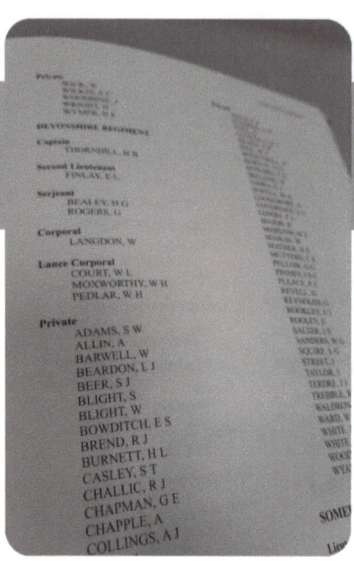

HERBERT BURNETT

Service Number: 1893
Rank: Private
1st / 4th Battalion
Devonshire Regiment
Born: December 1892
Died: 06 July 1916
Buried: Basra War Cemetery, Iraq

Herbert Lawrence Burnett was born in December 1892 and answered the call to serve King and country when war broke out in 1914.

He enlisted with the 4th Devonshire Regiment, heading overseas in October 1914 to India and then later to Mesopotamia (Iraq). After being involved in the significant attack on the Hai Salient, the Devonshire Regiment were involved with building roads and establishing the Tigris defences and lines of communication.

Herbert Burnett died from the effects of the extreme heat in Basra on 06 July 1916. He was just 24 years old and was buried in plot V. O. 15. at the Basra War Cemetery.

Sadly, this cemetery was largely destroyed in the early part of the 21st century due to political instability. All those buried and commemorated in Iraq are listed in a *Roll of Honour* and the *Basra War Memorial,* which does still exist.

Basra War Memorial, Iraq

JOHN BURTON

Service Number: 3/8092
Rank: Private
1st Battalion
Devonshire Regiment
Born: Unknown
Died: 10 March 1915
Buried: Ration Farm Annexe, Belgium

This is an interesting case of mistaken identity! Listed as R Burnett on the town's War Memorial, and 'Richard' on the stained-glass window in the church, there are no R Burnett's recorded within the Devonshire Regiment and no R Burnett's killed in any regiment in March 1915. However, a John Burton - brother of Mr J Burnett of 6 High Street, Bampton is recorded as having lost his life on 15 March 1915, and seeing as his name is missing from the memorial, it is likely that this is the correct person.

THOMAS BURNETT

Service Number: 200248
Rank: Private
2nd/ 4th Battalion
Devonshire Regiment
Born: 1886
Died: 14 July 1917
Buried: Madras (St Mary's) Cemetery, India

Born in 1886 to Mr & Mrs John Burnett of 6 High Street, Bampton, Thomas Nathaniel Burnett is the older brother of Herbert Burnett (who was killed in July 1916) and the likely nephew of John Burton, who was killed in March 1915.

The 2nd/4th Battalion were stationed in India when Thomas was involved in an accident where he fractured his skull and sadly succumbed to his injuries on 14 July 1917. He is buried in plot 18. 181. of the St. Mary's Cemetery in Madras.

FRANCIS CANDLER

Service Number: 50595
Rank: Lance Corporal
14th Battalion
Royal Warwickshire
Regiment
Born: 1899
Died: 27 September 1918
Commemorated: Vis-en-Artois Memorial, France

Francis John Candler was born in 1899 to Mr J & Mrs Candler of Castle Street, Bampton.

The 14th Battalion of the Royal Warwickshire Regiment was raised in September 1914 and it would seem that Francis enlisted as soon as he could. In November 1915, they landed at Boulogne-sur-Mer and stayed on the Western Front until November 1917, when they served six months in Italy before heading back to France in April 1918.

He was killed on 27 September 1918, just a few months before the 11 November armistice.

Francis John Candler was just 19 years old and his body was never found. He is commemorated on Panel 3 of the Vis-en-Artois Memorial.

The Vis-en-Artois Memorial stands behind the Vis-en-Artois Cemetery, just to the sout-east of Arras. Unveiled in 1930, it has the names of over 9,000 men who lost their lives in the area and who have no known grave.

Vis-en-Artois Memorial, France

WILLIAM COTTRELL

Service Number: 460040
Rank: Private
    44th Battalion
    Canadian Infantry
Born: 1886
Died: 09 January 1919
Buried: Wedmore Churchyard, UK

William Cottrell was born in 1886 to Annie Cottrell of 30 Brook Street, Bampton. He married Maria and they had at least one child Leslie William Cottrell (who was later killed in the Second World War).

William enlisted on the 24 August 1915 and embarked to Halifax, Canada for training. Once this was complete he boarded the *SS Olympic* and headed back to England in April 1916, transferring to the 44th Battalion and then made his way to northern France in August 1916. On the 25 October he received a gun shot wound to his lower left arm and was taken to Wimereux field hospital for treatment, before coming back home to Norfolk War Hospital and Auxilery hospital Great Yarmouth.

Wimereux field hospital

By this time, the family home was now at Church Villa, Wedmore in Somerset. Over the winter of 1916 / 1917 he continued his convalescing at Epsom hospital before he rejoined the 44th Battalion in March 1917.

The 44th Battalion remained in northern France, and a year and a half later on 30 September 1918, William was wounded again, this time to his lower leg.

The injury was bad enough for him to be invalided back to Britain and he was admitted to 1st Eastern General Hospital Cambridge on 31 October 1918.

William Cottrell died of his wounds on 09 January 1919. He was buried in St Mary Magdalene Churchyard, Wedmore.

St Mary Magdalene Church, Wedmore

CHARLES CURTIS

Service Number: 16042
Rank: Private
8th Battalion
Somerset Light Infantry
Born: March 1895
Died: 29 April 1917
Commemorated: Arras Memorial, France

Charles Thomas Curtis was born in March 1895 to William and Emma Curtis of Gander's Dairy, Bampton.

He enlisted with the 8th Battalion of the Somerset Light Infantry in October 1914 in Taunton and served with them on the western front.

On 28 April 1917, Charles Curtis was killed but his body was never recovered. He is commemorated on Panel 4 of the Arras Memorial in France, along with almost 35,000 others.

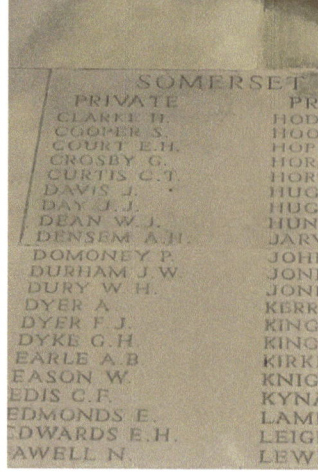

ARTHUR DAVEY

Service Number: 242223
Rank: Sergeant
  1st / 5th Battalion
  Somerset Light Infantry
Born: 1884
Died: 06 March 1919
Buried: Kantara War Cemetery, Egypt

Arthur John Davey was born in 1884 to Charles & Sarah Davey of Silver Street, Bampton. In 1907 he married Alice Maud Newbury and they had one child, named Cecil John.

He enlisted with the Somerset Light Infantry and was posted to Egypt in May 1917. He saw service in Palestine, Jerusalem and Damascus but sadly drowned in the Suez Canal in an accident on 06 March 1919.

A DUNSTER

Service Number:
Rank:
             Devonshire Regiment
Born:
Died:
Commemorated:

There is an *A Dunster* listed on the Bampton War Memorial, but not on the stained-glass window in the church. There are no records of an *A Dunster* with the Commonwealth War Graves Commission, so the full identity of this man remains unknown.

WILLIAM ESCOTT

Service Number: 43577
Rank: Private
   2nd Battalion
   South Lancashire Regiment
Born: 1884
Died: 29 April 1918
Buried: La Clytte Military Cemetery, Belgium

William Escott was born in 1884 to John and Harriet Escott, and was the brother of Mrs P Napper of 3 Frog Street, Bampton.

William enlisted at the beginning of the war with the South Lancashire Regiment and saw action in north France and Belgium. He was killed on 29 April 1918 and was buried in plot V. F. 3. of the La Clytte Military Ceremony in Belgium.

JAMES GAGE

Service Number: 267876
Rank: Private
   1st / 6th Battalion
   Devonshire Regiment
Born: Unknown
Died: 18 March 1917
Commemorated: Kirkee Memorial, India

James A. Gage was born in Bampton and was part of the territorial battalion of the Devonshire Regiment, based in Barnstaple.

The battalion landed in Karachi, Pakistan in November 1914. They became part of the 36th Indian Brigade and remained in the region for the next twelve months, before redeploying to Basra in January 1916. The battalion remained in Mesopotamia for the duration of the conflict.

On 18 March 1917, James A Gage was killed and is remembered alongside others of the Devonshire Regiment on Face C of the Kirkee Memorial in India.

The Kirkee Memorial in the town of Poona commemorates over 1800 men who lost their lives during the Great War as well as 700 graves.

W GARDENER

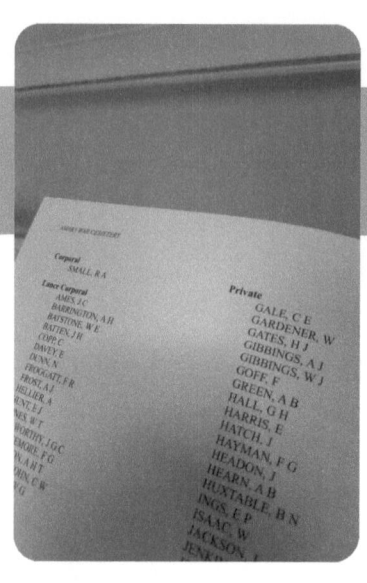

Service Number: 200749
Rank: Private
           Devonshire Regiment
Born: Unknown
Died: 21 August 1918
Buried: Amara War Cemetery, Iraq

Sadly, not much is known about W J Gardener. He was born in Bampton and like numerous other locals, joined the Devonshire Regiment when war broke out in 1914.

He was posted overseas as part of the Mesopotamian Expeditionary Force. The town of Amara became a hospital centre as the allies utilised the transport links the *River Tigris* offered, and it was here that he died on 21 August 1918.

The Amara War Cemetery contains over 4,500 graves, of which 3,500 are identified. The vast majority of these burials were brought to the cemetery after the First World War had finished from their initial resting places, right across the region.

However, in the 1930s all the headstones here were removed due to salt in the soil causing them to slowly deteriorate. Their names were then engraved on a large screen wall - detailing in which plot they rest.

W Gardener is buried in plot XIV. C. 11 at Amara.

Sadly, the political instability of the region means that visiting the cemetery itself is difficult.

A Roll of Honour, containing the names of all those identified at Amara, can be accessed at the Commonwealth War Graves Commission's headquarters in Maidenhead.

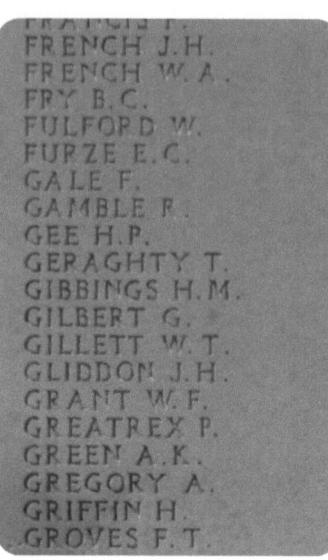

MICHAEL GIBBINGS

Service Number: 45677
Rank: Private
8th Battalion
Devonshire Regiment
Born: 1895
Died: 26 October 1917
Commemorated: Tyne Cot Memorial, Belgium

Michael Hubert Gibbings was born to Francis and Elizabeth Gibbings of Castle Street, Bampton in the autumn of 1895.

In the summer of 1914, with the world slowly heading towards an inevitable conflict, a number of new battalions were established and the 8th Battalion of the Devonshire Regiment was one of these. Michael joined up when it was formed in Exeter on 19 August 1914.

On 26 June 1915 they landed at Le Havre, France and stayed around the French / Belgium boarder for much of the war. Michael lost his life on 26 October 1917 - the opening day of the *Second Battle of Passchendaele*.

Michael Gibbings is commemorated on panel 38-40 of the Tyne Cot Memorial in Belgium. He was just 22 years old and his body was sadly, never found.

Tyne Cot, Belgium

WILLIAM GIBBINGS

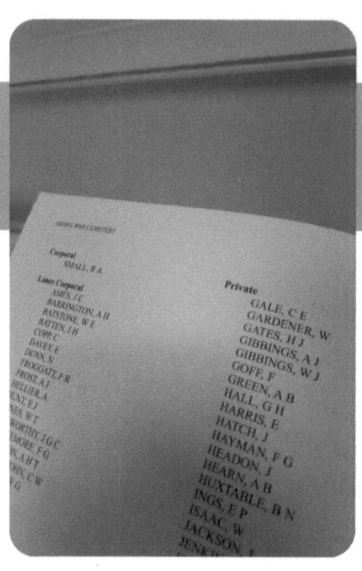

Service Number: 3732
Rank: Private
1st / 4th Battalion
Devonshire Regiment
Born: 1889
Died: 01 February 1917
Buried: Amara War Cemetery, Iraq

William John Gibbings was born in 1889 to John and Mary Gibbings of Tiverton New Road, Bampton. He married Ada Davey in the autumn of 1915 before being deployed overseas to Mesopotamia.

William Gibbings died on 01 February 1917 and is buried in plot XXI. K. 7. at the Amara War Cemetery in Iraq. Sadly, the political instability of the region means that visiting the cemetery itself is difficult, and in the 1930s all the headstones here were removed due to salt in the soil causing them to slowly deteriorate. Their names were then engraved on a large screen wall - detailing in which plot they rest. There is also a Roll of Honour, containing the names of all those identified at Amara, that can be accessed at the Commonwealth War Graves Commission's headquarters in Maidenhead.

ARTHUR GILLARD

Service Number: 8977
Rank: Private
1st Battalion
Devonshire Regiment
Born: 1889
Died: 17 December 1914
Commemorated: Menin Gate, Belgium

Arthur Gillard was born in 1889 to James and Anna Gillard of 5 West Street, Bampton. Arthur was already a regular soldier when the First World War broke out and was part of the *British Expeditionary Force* to land at Le Havre in August 1914.

He lost his life at Ypres on 17 December 1914. His body was never recovered, and he is commemorated on panel 21 at the Menin Gate, Belgium.

JOHN GREENSLADE

Service Number: 1482
Rank: Private
  1st / 4th Battalion
  Devonshire Regiment
Born: 1890
Died: 03 December 1915
Buried: Kut War Cemetery, Iraq

John Thomas Greenslade was born in 1890 to Thomas and Emma Greenslade of Wind Whistle, Bampton. He enlisted with the Devonshire regiment and was sent overseas to Mesopotamia in the autumn of 1915.

He sadly lost his life on 03 December 1915 - one of three brothers from the town to do so.

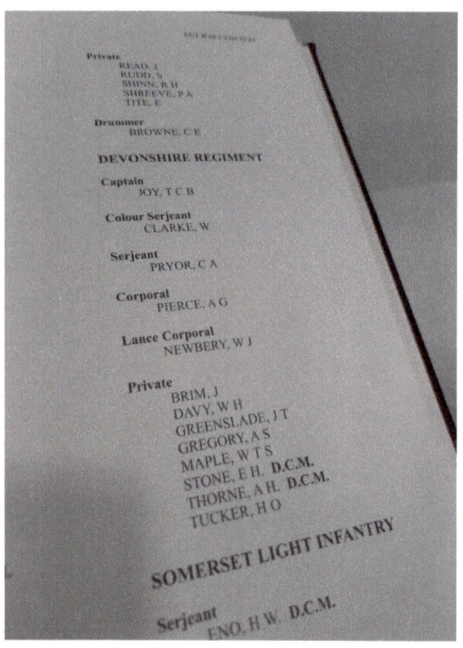

John Thomas Greenslade was buried at plot L. 17. of the Kut War Cemetery, Iraq.

The cemetery was established on the northern edge of the town between October 1915 and May 1916 and contains the graves of 420 commonwealth soldiers. There is also a Roll of Honour containing the names of all those buried at Kut, at the Commonwealth War Graves Commission's headquarters in Maidenhead.

REGINALD GREENSLADE

Service Number: 9705
Rank: Corporal
1st Battalion
Somerset Light Infantry
Born: 1894
Died: 23 August 1915
Buried: Mesnil Ridge Cemetery, France

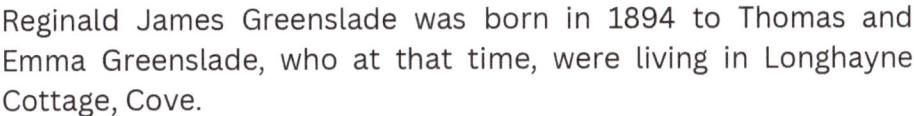

Reginald James Greenslade was born in 1894 to Thomas and Emma Greenslade, who at that time, were living in Longhayne Cottage, Cove.

He was already part of the regular army at the outbreak of the war and was sent over to France in August 1914. He was the first of three brothers from the town to lose his life in the conflict, being killed on 23 August 1915. He was just 21 years old.

Reginald is buried in plot J. 1. at the Mesnil Ridge Cemetery, France.

WILLIAM GREENSLADE

Service Number: 11394
Rank: Corporal
  7th Battalion
  Somerset Light Infantry
Born: 1892
Died: 30 November 1917
Commemorated: Cambrai Memorial, France

William Charles Greenslade was born in 1892 to Thomas and Emma Greenslade of Longhayne Cottage, Cove.

He served with the Somerset Light Infantry during the Great War and lost his life on 30 November 1917 during the Battle of Cambrai (20 November - 03 December 1917).

William's body was never recovered and he is commemorated, alongside the names of over 7,000 other men who have no known grave from this battle, on Panel 4 and 5 of the Cambrai Memorial in France.

EDMUND HANCOCK

Service Number: 16591
Rank: Private
    8th Battalion
    Devonshire Regiment
Born: 1886
Died: 12 July 1916
Buried: Bronfay Farm Military Cemetery, France

Edmund Hancock was born to James and Rhoda Hancock of Castle Street, Bampton in 1886. He joined the newly formed 8th Battalion of the Devonshire Regiment in Exeter on 19 August 1914.

On 26 June 1915 they landed at Le Havre, France and stayed around the French / Belgium boarder for much of the war. Edmund was killed on 12 July 1916 at Bray-sur-Somme and is buried in plot II. A. 13. at the Bronfay Farm Military Cemetery.

FREDERICK HUTCHINGS

Service Number: 18990
Rank: Private
9th Battalion
Devonshire Regiment
Born: Unknown
Died: 05 July 1916
Buried: St. Sever Cemetery, France

Frederick Hutchings was born to Thomas and Mary Hutchings of 3 Tiverton Road.

In the summer of 1914, with the world slowly heading towards an inevitable conflict, a number of new battalions were established and the 9th Battalion of the Devonshire Regiment was one of these. Frederick joined up when it was formed in Exeter on 15 September 1914.

On 28 July 1915 they landed at Le Havre, France and stayed around the French / Belgium boarder for much of the war.

After seeing action in the *Battle of Loos*, they fought in the infamous *Battle of the Somme*, and it was during this offensive that Frederick was injured. He was taken to the huge hospital centre at Rouen, away from the front line, but he sadly lost his life on 05 July 1916.

Frederick Hutchings is buried in plot A. 23. 17. at the St. Sever Cemetery in Rouen, France.

ALFRED HUTTER

Service Number: 3/7286
Rank: Private
    1st Battalion
    Devonshire Regiment
Born: 1878
Died: 13 April 1916
Buried: Faubourg D'Amiens Cemetery, Arras, France

Alfred Ernest Hutter was born in 1878 to Charles and Susan Hutter of Lark Cottage, Halcombe Rogus.

He was married to Sarah and they lived at 18 Frog Street, Bampton. He was already a regular soldier when the First World War broke out and the 1st Battalion, who were in Jersey at the time, soon deployed to Le Havre as part of the *British Expeditionary Force*, in August 1914. The battalion fought in the First and Second Battles of Ypres.

In January 1916 they transferred to the 95th Brigade of the 5th Division and in March 1916 they took over a section of the front line near Vimy Ridge, not far from Arras.

It was whilst holding this line, that Alfed was killed on 13 April 1916 and is buried at plot I. A. 39. at the Faubourg D'Amiens Cemetery in Arras, France, which is the final resting place of over 2,600 men from the Great War.

ARTHUR KERSLAKE

Service Number: 11214
Rank: Lance Corporal
       1st Battalion
       Devonshire Regiment
Born: 1890
Died: 25 September 1916
Commemorated: Thiepval Memorial, France

Arthur Kerslake was born in 1890 to Robert and Elizabeth Kerslake of Mill Head. He was already a regular soldier when the First World War broke out and the 1st Battalion, who were in Jersey at the time, soon deployed to Le Havre as part of the British Expeditionary Force, in August 1914. Whilst on leave that winter, he married his sweetheart, Emma Western in December 1914.

Arthur was killed on 25 September 1916, aged 26. His body was never recovered and he is commemorated on Pier & Face 1 C of the Thiepval Memorial, France.

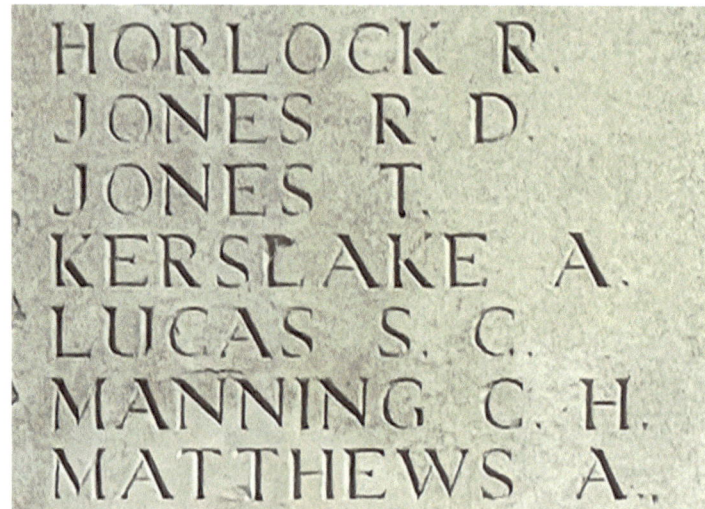

HORACE KINGDOM

Service Number: 30429
Rank: Private
  1st Battalion
  Devonshire Regiment
Born: 1896
Died: 06 May 1917
Buried: Lapugnoy Military Cemetery, France

Horace Donald Kingdom was born in 1896 to William and Catherine in Stoodleigh, Devon. The family moved to 125 Brook Street and Horace became an agricultural worker.

The outbreak of the war saw Horace sign up just as soon as he could. On 06 May 1917 he sadly lost his life at the age of just 21. He is buried in plot IV. B. 4. of the Lapugnoy Military Cemetery, France.

RICHARD LUGG

Service Number: 44446
Rank: Private
   2nd / 4th Battalion
   Royal Berkshire Regiment
Born: 1900
Died: 07 June 1918
Buried: St. Venant-Robecq Road British Cemetery, France

Richard George Lugg was born in 1900 to Richard and Charlotte Lugg. His father died and his mother remarried, becoming Charlotte Jefford, and they lived at 1 Fore Street, Bampton.

The 2nd / 4th Battalion was an additional territorial regiment formed after September 1914. They were sent over to the Western Front in the summer of 1916.

Richard joined as soon as he was old enough and the battalion spent the duration of the war along the front line.

Sadly, Richard died on 07 June 1918 aged just 18 years old. He is buried in plot IV. C. 20. of the St. Venant-Robecq Road British Cemetery in France. Just under 500 commonwealth burials can be found here.

TOM MANTLE

Service Number: 40180
Rank: Private
   1st / 5th Battalion
   Gloucestershire Regiment
Born: 1888
Died: 03 November 1918
Buried: Landrecies British Cemetery, France

Tom Mantle was born in 1888 to Tom and Martha Mantle of Clayhanger. He married Gertrude in 1916 and they lived at 1 Haddon View, King's Brompton, Dulverton. He joined the Gloucestershire regiment, who served in France and Italy, before returning to France and taking part in *The Final Advance in Picardy* in the autumn of 1918. Tom was killed during this attack on 03 November 1918. He is buried in plot A. 44. at the Landrecies British Cemetery in France.

GILBERT NOTT

Service Number: 4153
Rank: Private
   3rd / 4th Battalion
   Devonshire Regiment
Born: 1895
Died: 03 May 1916
Buried: St Michael's Church, Bampton

Gilbert Charles Nott was born in 1895 to William and Eleanor Nott of 9 Brook Street, Bampton. After signing up to the Devonshire Regiment, he was injured and taken to a hospital in Winchester, where he sadly died on 03 May 1916. Buried in St Michael's Church graveyard, he is incorrectly listed as A. C. Nott on the town's war memorial, but correctly listed as G. C. Nott on the plaque inside the church.

SYDNEY PARSONS

Service Number: 8328
Rank: Sergeant
   1st Battalion
   Devonshire Regiment
Born: 1889
Died: 23 April 1917
Commemorated: Arras Memorial, France

Sydney Parsons was born in 1889 to John and Emma Parsons of Turnpike Gatehouse, Shillingford. He was already a regular soldier in the 1st battalion of the Devonshire regiment when war broke out in 1914.

He was killed on 23 April 1917 aged 28. His body was never recovered and he is commemorated on Bay 4 of the Arras Memorial in France.

WILLIAM PARSONS

Service Number: 6684
Rank: Corporal
　　　　1st Battalion
　　　　Devonshire Regiment
Born: 1882
Died: 04 October 1917
Buried: Tyne Cot Cemetery, Belgium

William Parsons was born in 1882 to John and Emma Parsons of Turnpike Gatehouse, Shillingford. Like his younger brother Sydney, he was already a regular soldier in the 1st battalion of the Devonshire regiment when war broke out in 1914.

The 1st Battalion were in Jersey in the summer of 1914 and soon deployed to Le Havre as part of the British Expeditionary Force, in the August of that year.

He was killed on 04 October 1917 aged 35 and is buried in plot LXIII. D. 2. of the Tyne Cot Cemetery in Belgium.

The cemetery is the largest Commonwealth War Cemetery in the world in terms of burials - with over 11,900 graves. Just over 8,300 of these are unidentified. The Tyne Cot memorial is also here, commemorating over 35,000 commonwealth soldiers who lost their lives in the Ypres Salient after August 1917, but have no known grave.

AMARA WAR CEMETERY

FREDERICK RABJOHNS

Service Number: 2074
Rank: Private
2nd / 4th Battalion
Devonshire Regiment
Born: 1895
Died: 06 February 1917
Buried: Amara War Cemetery, Iraq

Frederick John Rabjohns was born in 1895 to John and Elizabeth Rabjohns of Wind Whistle, Cove, before they later moved to Tiverton New Road.

Frederick was a territorial soldier before the Great War broke out and so was one of the first to be deployed abroad - heading to India in the autumn of 1914. He was part of the advance on *Kut,* but was killed in action during this assault.

He was killed on 06 February 1917 aged 22 and is buried in plot XXVI. G. 6. of the Amara War Cemetery in Iraq.

Over 4500 men are buried here, but in the 1930s all the headstones were removed due to salt in the soil causing them to deteriorate. Their names were then engraved on a large screen wall, as well as being recorded in a Roll of Honour at the Commonwealth War Grave Commission's Head Office.

His brother, George, also served during the conflict but survived.

	HEARN, ...
	HUXTABLE, B N
	INGS, E P
	ISAAC, W
	JACKSON, J
	JENKINS, E
	JONES, R C
	JOY, A
	JUPE, F
	KENNARD, S G
	KENWOOD, A
	LANE, A
	LIVERTON, G
	LOCK, C
	LOCK, F
	LYONS, H J
	MAY, J G
	MILES, A J
	MILLS, A E
	MORTIMORE, A
	McKENZIE, J V
	NORTHMORE, F W
	OLDREY, G
	PALMER, J
	POTTER, J E
	POWELL, A E
	PUGSLEY, A J
	PURSE, F G
	PURSE, H
	RABJOHNS, F J
	RENDELL, J
	RENDLE, R
	RICE, F E
	RICHARDS, F C
	ROSS, J H
	RUSSELL, W J
	SAMWAYS, A
	SANSO...

Privates:
ALFORD, ...
ARNOLD, W
BALL, F
BALL, S ...
BASTARD, J L
BASTONE, W D
BATE, ...
BEER, A J
BEER, F
BENBROOK, W
BENNETT, W R
BOARD, W F M
BOWDEN, F C
BOWDEN, J
BOYCE, J R
BRAUND, P
BROWN, B H
BUCKINGHAM, W H
CARTMELL, W
...RKE, L
...SON, E F
...ILL, F
..., F W
... W H
... W A
... W

ERNEST SERENGER

Service Number: 7461
Rank: Corporal
           1st Battalion
           Devonshire Regiment
Born: 1881
Died: 13 September 1916
Buried: Serre Road Cemetery, France

Ernest Scherzinger was born in Germany in 1881, before moving to Bampton with his parents when he was very young.

He was already in the army prior to the outbreak of World War One and was soon deployed to Le Havre as part of the British Expeditionary Force, in the August of 1914. They spent the duration of the conflict on the Western Front and saw action in the First and Second Battles of Ypres, Vimy Ridge and The Somme.

Ernest was killed on 13 September 1916 aged 35 years old. He was buried in plot XXVI. J. 2. in the Serre Road Cemetery Number 2 in France.

Due to the large, and understandable, anti-German feeling in the country at the time, his family used the anglicised version of their surname (Serenger) on the town's war memorial.

Serre Road Cemetery No. 2 sits towards the northern point of the allied offensive on the first day of the *Battle of the Somme*.

Situated near *Hébuterne* in the Pas-de-Calais region of France, over 7,000 men from the Commonwealth are buried here, although sadly, nearly 5,000 of these are unidentified. Casualties from Britain, Australia, Canadia, New Zealand, South Africa and Germany have their final resting place here.

SYDNEY STEVENS

Service Number: 3/7003
Rank: Private
  1st Battalion
  Devonshire Regiment
Born: 1892
Died: 18 May 1915
Buried: Spoilbank Cemetery, Belgium

Sydney Charles Stevens was born in 1892 to William and Ellen Stevens of 13 Pinkstone's Court, Tiverton.

They later moved to Bampton and when Sydney left school he got a job at Bampton Quarries.

The outbreak of the Great War provided many men with an opportunity to earn steady money, as well providing them with a sense of adventure, and Sydney enlisted in August 1914.

The 1st battalion spent the duration of the conflict on the Western Front and it was during the *Second Battle of Ypres* that Sydney lost his life in the trenches to the south-east of Ypres.

He was killed on 18 May 1915 and is buried in plot I. C. 2. of the Spoilbank Cemetery in Belgium.

Located a few miles south of the Ypres (Leper) town centre, Spoilbank Cemetery is also sometimes referred to as *Chester Farm Lower Cemetery* or *Gordon Terrace Cemetery*.

The cemetery contains just over 500 burials and commemorations of those who lost their lives on the battlefields of Ypres. Designed by *Sir Edwin Lutyens*, over 100 of the burials are sadly unidentified.

FELIX TARR

Service Number: 955
Rank: Private
          West Somerset Yeomanry
Born: 1889
Died: 16 October 1915
Buried: East Mudros Military Cemetery, Greece

Felix Tarr was born to George and Bessie Tarr of Exbridge, Bampton.

The outbreak of the Great War provided many men with an opportunity to earn steady money, as well providing them with a sense of adventure, and Felix enlisted with the West Somerset Yeomanry.

In September 1915 they sailed from Liverpool on the *Olympic* heading for Gallipoli. They landed on 09 October 1915 at *Suvla bay*, and it was during this time that Felix got injured.

He was evacuated to a hospital ship but sadly died of his injuries on 16 October 1915. He is buried in plot III. B. 47. at the East Mudros Military Cemetery on the Greek island of Lemnos.

It was reported in the Tiverton Gazette on 02 November 1915 that the flag on Brushford Church was flown at half mast in his honour.

ISAAC THORNE

Service Number: 3034
Rank: Private
2nd / 4th Battalion
Devonshire Regiment
Born: 1874
Died: 10 August 1915
Buried: Madras (St. Mary's) Cemetery, India

Isaac Thorne was born in 1874 to Ian and Lucy Thorne in Cardiff. In 1896, he married Laura Escott of 56 Brook Street, Bampton and they lived at Bampton Down.

The 2nd / 4th battalion were formed at Exeter in September 1914 and were then deployed to India in the autumn of that year. They were mainly charged with carrying out internal security and logistic duties, with Isaac working at Fort St. George in Madras.

Isaac Thorne died on 10 August 1915 aged 41 years old - likely from illness or disease.

He is buried at plot 18. 171. at the Madras (St. Mary's) Cemetery in Chennai, India, along with over 850 other Commonwealth servicemen.

A further 1,000 names are listed on the *Madras 1914–1918 War Memorial* that is also situated in the cemetery.

FRANK TOOZE

Service Number: 19408
Rank: Private
7th Battalion
Somerset Light Infantry
Born: 1896
Died: 20 November 1917
Buried: Rocquigny-Equancourt Road British Cemetery, France

Frank Tooze was born in 1896 to Mr J and Mrs Selina Tooze of Petton Dairies, Bampton.

The 7th battalion of the Somerset Light Infantry was formed in Taunton in August 1914 and Frank signed up for king and country just as soon as he could - no doubt buoyed by the sense of adventure that would be something very different to working in the dairy.

The 7th battalion were deployed to the Western Front in July 1915 and stayed in the area for the duration of the conflict.

Frank was killed on 20 November 1917, aged just 21. He is buried at plot II. D. 2. at the Rocquigny-Equancourt Road British Cemetery in the countryside to the east of Amiens in the Somme area.

Over 2,000 Commonwealth soldiers are buried here, along with nearly 200 German soldiers and 10 French civilians.

HENRY TUCKER

Service Number: 345706
Rank: Lance Corporal
16th Battalion
Devonshire Regiment
Born: 1898
Died: 18 October 1918
Buried: Cambrin Military Cemetery, France

Henry John Tucker was born in 1898 to Henry and Elizabeth Tucker of Fleeds, Clayhanger, Bampton. He enlisted with the Devonshire regiment and after completing his training, joined up with the 16th battalion who served in Sinai and Palestine before heading to the Western Front. It was here, that Henry was killed on 18 October 1918 - only a month before the armistice. He was just 20 years old. Henry Tucker is buried in plot Q. 20. at the Cambrin Military Cemetery, France.

THOMAS VICKERY

Service Number: 810244
Rank: Sergeant
232nd Brigade
Royal Field Artillery
Born: 1894
Died: 24 April 1917
Buried: Duisans British Cemetery, France

Thomas William Vickery was born in 1894 to Depot Sergeant-Major T. and Mrs Vickery of Prospect House, Bampton. Whilst serving with the 232nd Brigade of the Royal Field Artillery he was seriously wounded by shrapnel to his stomach and died at the 8th Casualty Clearing Station in Etrun, a few miles to the west of Arras. Thomas is buried in plot III. D. 36. of the Duisans British Cemetery in France.

FREDERICK WARE

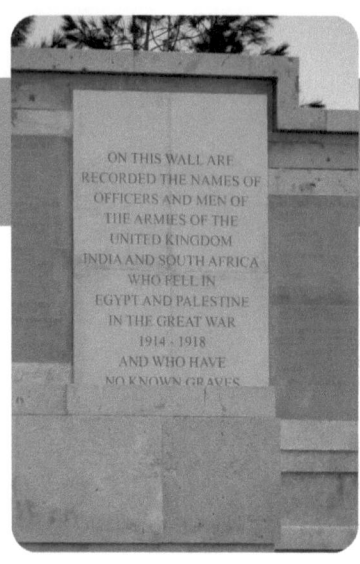

Service Number: 20799
Rank: Corporal
5th Battalion
Devonshire Regiment
Born: 1894
Died: 23 November 1917
Commemorated: Jerusalem Memorial, Israel

Frederick Ware was born in 1894 to Mr G & Mrs C Ware of 2 Back Street, Bampton.

He enlisted with the 5th Battalion of the Devonshire regiment, and they landed in Karachi, Pakistan on 11 November 1914 in order to relieve existing units so they could return to the Western Front.

They then formed part of the *Egyptian Expeditionary Force* and arrived in Suez on 04 April 1917, heading up to Palestine and Gaza.

On 21 November 1917, there was fierce fighting in the Judean Hills, west Jerusalem, and on 23 November they took part in an attack on *El Jib* that ran into Turkish artillery and machine gun fire with Frederick being one of the casualties.

Frederick Ware is commemorated on panel 15 of the Jerusalem Memorial, which is inside the grounds of the Jerusalem War Cemetery.

CORPORAL
BACK W.
SKINNER A.

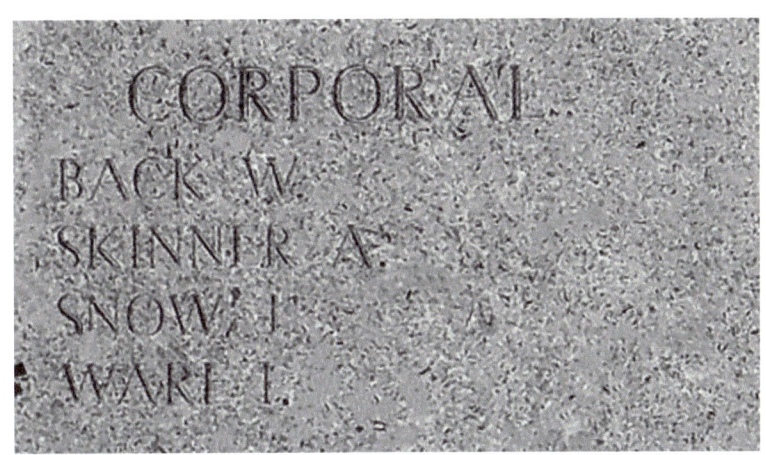

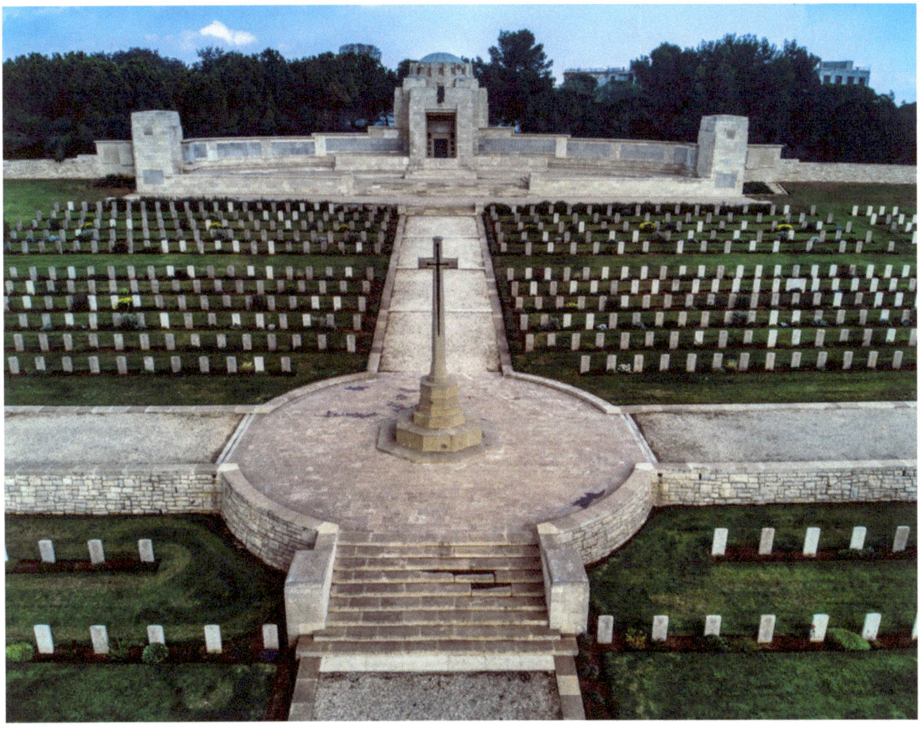

CHARLEY TOZE

Service Number: 7624
Rank: Private
   1st Battalion
   Devonshire Regiment
Born: Unknown
Died: 24 October 1914
Commemorated: Le Touret Memorial, France

The name of Charley Toze was added onto the Bampton War Memorial in 2015, when relatives researching their family tree noticed it was missing.

He lost his life on 24 October 1914 and is commemorated on Panel 8 and 9 of the Le Touret Memorial in France - along with over 13,000 others who fought in the area and who have no known grave.

ANKETELL MOUTRAY READ VC

Service Number:
Rank: Captain
1st Battalion
Northamptonshire Regiment
Born: 27 October 1884
Died: 25 September 1915
Buried: Dud Corner Cemetery, Loos, France

Anketell Moutray Read VC was born on 27 October 1884 to Colonel John & Mrs E Moutray Read of Beaumont House, 56 Shurdington Road, Leckhampton, Cheltenham. He was educated at *Glyngarth School*, Cheltenham, before going to the *United Services College*, Westward Ho! and later becoming a Gentleman Cadet at the *Royal Military College*, Sandhurst.

Anketell joined the Gloucester Regiment as a 2nd Lieutenant in 1903, serving in India, before transferring to the Northamptonshire regiment in 1911. His battalion landed at *Le Havre* in August 1914 and fought in the *Battle of Mons* and the *Battle of Aisne* - in which he was severely wounded. He was promoted to Captain in March 1915 and returned to his battalion.

Anketell was killed by a sniper on 25 September 1915 - the opening day of the *Battle of Loos* - and is buried in plot VII. F. 19. at the Dud Corner Cemetery. He was posthumously awarded a Victoria Cross (VC) for *'most conspicuous bravery. Although partially gassed, Captain Read went out several times in order to rally parties of different units... he led them back into the firing line, and, utterly regardless of danger, moved freely about encouraging them under a withering fire. He was mortally wounded while carrying out this gallant work.'*

There is a commemorative plaque in St Michael & All Angels church.

A commemorative paving slab was added at the base of the Bampton War Memorial in October 2015.

HUGH LEONARD ACLAND TROYTE

Service Number:
Rank: Lieutenant Colonel
           4th Battalion
           Devonshire Regiment
Born: 1870
Died: 17 April 1918
Buried: Berguette Churchyard, France

Hugh Leonard Acland Troyte was born in 1870 to Colonel Charles Arthur William Troyte and Katherine Mary Walrond of Huntsham Court.

He lived at Little Court, Berrow, Somerset with his wife Helen Jessie Acland Troyte.

Hugh was in the 1st / 4th battalion of the Devonshire Regiment, seeing action in Mesopotamia and India, before he was invalided back home.

A commemorative plaque in St Michael & All Angels church.

In 1916, Hugh was well enough to return to action and this time was attached to the General Staff on the Western Front. It was during this time that Hugh was killed on 17 April 1916 in the small French village of Berguette, whilst evacuating civilians from the area. He is buried in plot D. 2. of the Berguette Churchyard in France.

He is remembered on the war memorial in the village of Huntsham but also on a plaque in St Michael & All Angels Church in Bampton.

STANLEY ALDERMAN

Service Number: 5620037
Rank: Gunner
           Royal Artillery
           4 Maritime Regiment
Born: 1922
Died: 09 May 1941
Commemorated: Plymouth Naval Memorial

Stanley John Alderman was born in 1922 to Ernest Allen Alderman and Ethel Maud Alderman of Bampton.

The Second World War broke out when he was 17 and Stanley joined the Royal Artillery (R. A.) as a gunner - being one of many men responsible for manning the defensive armament aboard Merchant Navy ships along with the Royal Navy D.E.M.S.

The 4th Maritime Regiment R.A. was based at Southport, Lancashire.

Stanley John Alderman lost his life on 09 May 1941, at the age of just 19 years old. He is commemorated on column 2, panel 62 of the Plymouth Naval Memorial, along with 23,000 others lost at sea and who have no known grave.

PLUMRIDGE C.
TAYLOR J.
WHITE T.G.

GUNNER

ALDERMAN S.J.
BARKER W.
BASS T.
BATTY J.
BRADFORD W.
BROADHURST G.

VICTOR BROWN

Service Number: 964042
Rank: Sergeant
14 Squadron Royal Air Force Volunteer Reserve
Born: Unkown
Died: 10 March 1943
Commemorated: Alamein Memorial, Egypt

Victor Brown was born in Bampton and joined 14 Squadron of the Royal Air Force Volunteer Reserve. The squadron was briefly deployed to Ismailia and then Amman at the beginning of the Second World War. They soon relocated to Port Sudan in readiness for operations against Italian forces.

By October 1941, 14 Squadron moved to operations in the Western Desert - taking part in Operation Crusader, before being part of the mass retreat towards El Alemein.

In May 1942 the Squadron converted to using Martin B26 Marauder's, carrying out armed torpedo reconnaissance and naval mine-laying sorties over the Mediterranean, whilst also doing low-level coastal reconnaissance across the Mediterranean, Tyrrhenian and Adriatic Seas.

On 10 March 1943, the tail fin of the plane Victor was in snapped off during flight, making it uncontrollable. The Marauder FK154/K crashed into the Bay of Algiers killing nine.

Sadly, only two bodies were recovered from the crash.

Victor Brown's body was never recovered.

He is commemorated on column 270 of the Alamein Memorial in Egypt along with nearly 12,000 other allied commonwealth servicemen who lost their lives in the area and who have no known grave.

KENNETH BURNETT

Service Number: 1701051
Rank: Leading Aircraftman
Royal Air Force
Born: 1923
Died: 31 July 1945
Buried: Irvinestown Churchyard, Northern Ireland

Kenneth John Burnett was born to Leonard Cyril and Priscilla Burnett of Bampton. He joined the Royal Air Force and was stationed in Northern Ireland. Sadly, Kenneth drowned whilst swimming in Lough Erne, he was 22 years old. He is buried in grave 68, plot 2 of the Irvinestown Church of Ireland Churchyard.

FELIX COTTRELL

Service Number: D/L904Y
Rank: Petty Officer Steward
Royal Navy
HMS Drake
Born: 1897
Died: 24 November 1940
Buried: Cardonald Cemetery, Glasgow

Felix Cottrell was born to Albert and Elizabeth Cottrell of Bampton, before moving to St. Budeaux, Plymouth when he married Florence. They had two sons: Peter and Michael.

Felix was a member of the Royal Navy before the Second World War began, and during the conflict was working as a Petty Officer Steward. This was a non-commissioned officer role responsible for a whole host of welfare issues such as catering, accommodation and social areas. He was stationed at HMS Drake - a shore establishment in Plymouth.

In the Autumn of 1940, Felix went to the Glasgow suburb of Clydebank to assist with the docks there. Like Plymouth, the port city of Glasgow was a big Luftwaffe target and on the night of 24 November 1940 it experienced a major air raid with heavy bombing and incendiary attacks during the night.

It was during this attack that Felix Cottrell lost his life. He was 43 years old.

Felix Cottrell is buried in Section E, Joint Grave 5, at the Cardonald Cemetery in Glasgow.

GILBERT COTTRELL

Service Number: 1350378
Rank: Flight Sergeant
582 Squadron Royal Air Force Volunteer Reserve
Born: 1921
Died: 15 June 1944
Buried: Coxyde Military Cemetery, Belgium.

Gilbert Valentine Cottrell was born to Samuel James and Eliza Anne Cottrell of Bampton, in 1921. He married Marjorie Ellen Cottrell of West Cross, Glamorgan.

582 Squadron was based at *RAF Little Staughton* and was part of the *Pathfinder Force* - marking targets for other bomber squadrons to hit later. Mainly flying Lancaster bombers, they were involved in numerous bombing raids over enemy territory.

On 15 June 1944, a little over a week after the D-Day landings, Gilbert and his crew boarded their Avro Lancaster III, ND714, at Little Staughton for a nighttime raid. They were one of a staggering 330 aircraft to take off that evening and attack the German railway infrastructure in and around the Normandy area. All the targets were covered in cloud and the attack achieved mixed results. Four aircraft were lost - with Gilbert's Lancaster crashing south-west of Adinkerke in Belgium. German records show that the aircraft was shot down by a night-fighter piloted by Oblt. Werner Hopf of 8./NJG5.

Gilbert Valentine is buried in Coll. grave V. H. 2-5 at the Coxyde Military Cemetery in Belgium, along with over 1,600 other servicemen from the First and Second World Wars.

An Avro Lancaster at the Shuttleworth Military Pageant 2013

Coxyde Military Cemetery, Belgium

G EVANS

Service Number:
Rank: Royal Air Force Volunteer Reserve
Born:
Died:
Buried:

There is a *G Evans* listed on the Bampton War Memorial as having served with the Royal Air Force Volunteer Reserve. In researching this book, we are unable to clarify which *G Evans* this man is, so his full identity remains unknown.

REGINALD FLOYDE

Service Number: 860686
Rank: Gunner
Royal Artillery
3 Field Regiment
Born: 1918
Died: 12 June 1942
Commemorated: Alamein Memorial, Egypt.

Reginald Thomas Floyde was born in Bampton and served with the 3 Field Regiment of the Royal Artillery. They saw service in North Africa and on the 12 June 1942, Reginald lost his life there.

Reginald Floyde's body was never recovered. He is commemorated on column 35 of the Alamein Memorial in Egypt along with nearly 12,000 other allied commonwealth servicemen who lost their lives in the area and who have no known grave. He is listed as *R G Floyd* on the Bampton War Memorial.

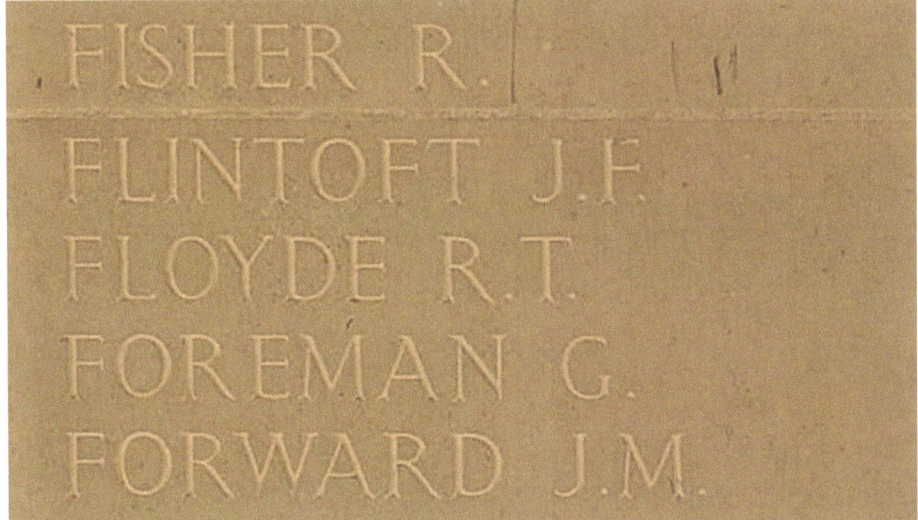

SYDNEY JONES

Service Number: 5608685
Rank: Warrant Officer (Class II)
    2nd Battalion
    Devonshire Regiment
Born: 1901
Died: 31 July 1943
Buried: Catania War Cemetery, Italy.

Sydney John Jones was born in 1901 in Bampton. He married Mabel Maria Jones of St. Thomas', Exeter.

He joined the Devonshire regiment during the inter-war period and rose to the rank of Warrant Officer (Second Class).

Left: A photograph of Sydney when he first enlisted.

The 2ⁿᵈ battalion were stationed on Malta as part of the 1st Malta Infantry Brigade and played their part in defending the island during the war - particularly during the siege (June 1940 - November 1942).

After this, they joined the 8th Army in North Africa and then participated in the invasion of Sicily in 1943.

It was during this time that Sydney lost his life.

He is buried in plot I. J. 34. of the Catania War Cemetery in Sicily, Italy, along with 2,000 other servicemen. He was 42 years old.

P HUTCHINGS

Service Number: S/5621348
Rank: Private
Royal Army Service Corps
Born: 1919
Died: 25 May 1947
Buried: St Michael & All Angels churchyard, Bampton

P Hutchings was born in 1919 to Mr & Mrs W. H. Hutchings of Bampton. Not much is known about his life or service, but judging by the date he died, it is likely it was as a result of injuries he received during the Second World War. He is buried in plot A. 19. of the St Michael & All Angels churchyard in Bampton.

EDWARD KENNARD

Service Number:
Rank: Lieutenant-Commander
Royal Navy
HMS Odyssey
Born: 1912
Died: 03 May 1945
Commemorated: Portsmouth Naval Memorial, UK.

Edward Walter Kennard was born in 1912 to Captain M. A. Kennard and Mrs F. W. Kennard of Bampton. During the Second World War, he was stationed at HMS Odyssey, and sadly lost his life on 03 May 1945.

He is commemorated on Panel 88 Column 2 of the Portsmouth Naval Memorial.

WILLIAM MOGRIDGE

Service Number: D/JX 254855
Rank: Able Seaman
Royal Navy
HMS Sultan
Born: 1913
Died: 25 August 1945
Buried: Jakarta War Cemetery, Indonesia.

William Ronald Mogridge was born in 1913 to Henry and Lillian Mogridge. He married Edith Mary and they lived in Bampton. He was killed on 25 August 1945 having been based at *HMS Sultan*. At this time (1945-1947) , *HMS Sultan* was a shore establishment based at Keppel Harbour, Singapore. William was buried in plot 1. E. 4. of the Jakarta War Cemetery, Indonesia.

A view of Keppel Harbour, Singapore

Jakarta War Cemetery, Indonesia

J PARTRIDGE

Service Number:
Rank:

Born:
Died:
Buried:

At the time of writing, we are unable to clarify with *J Partridge* from the *Commonwealth War Graves Commission* records this is.

FREDERICK WOODMAN

Service Number: 5621147
Rank: Serjeant
Royal Artillery
22 Anti-Tank Regiment
Born: 1922
Died: 07 April 1945
Commemorated: Rangoon Memorial, Myanmar

Frederick William Woodman was born in 1922 to Mr and Mrs R Woodman of Bampton. He served with the 22 Anti-Tank Regiment and was killed on 07 April 1945.

He is remembered on Face 2 of the Rangoon Memorial in Myanmar - formerly Burma.

BAMPTON REMEMBERS

In researching and creating this book, it was important to involve the local community as much as possible - and the Year 5 and 6 children at Bampton Primary School embarked on the *Bampton Remembers Project* in the autumn of 2024.

The pupils visited the War Memorial and church, and in their quest for finding out as much as they could, asked the wider community for any information they might have about the men.

The pupils received the background research that would later be used for creating this book, and then used their writing skills to create biographies of the men on the war memorial, as well as producing some rather poignant artwork.

The pupils led a Remembrance Day service at the War Memorial on 11 November 2024, with the whole school and wider members of the community attending.

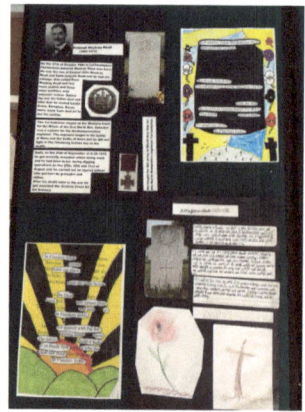

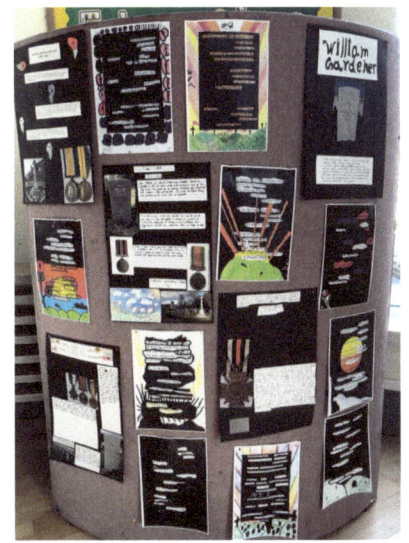

ACKNOWLEDGEMENTS

There are a number of people who need thanking for their help in making this project become a reality.

Tony Emptage for his hard work in locating the grave photographs; Nele Bille, Nigel Stevens and Lucie Balin from the Commonwealth War Graves Commission in helping to source photographs of each cemetery - and The Worldwide Operational Staff of the Commonwealth War Graves Commission (listed as CWGC below); All at Bampton Primary School for their support and enthusiasm for the project, especially Lully Newman and Mark Narramore - and of course the year 5 and 6 cohort who took great pride in honouring the men of their town.

With thanks to the Year 5 & 6 children at Bampton Primary School:
Patrick Barcoe, Lucas Bray, Tyler Domican, Jack Giorgione, Thomas Hill, Rosie Howard, Cassie Hughes, Imogen Hutter, Kodi Keating-Knight, Max Morgan, Michael Parker, Fennick Platt, Harry Pook, Ellora-Jasmine Roberts, Ella Standford, Toby Vigus, Robyn Ware and Craig Keating.

Photograph credits:

Front Cover (Clockwise from top left) Archie Needs, A Powell-Thomas, DJ Stanto, Geert Brouckaert; Page 7 A Powell-Thomas (4); Page 8 A Powell-Thomas (4); Page 9 A Powell-Thomas (3); Page 10 Hugh Waters; Page 11 Wernervc; Page 12 Nigel Stevens, CWGC; Page 13 CWGC (2); Page 14 CWGC; Page 15 CWGC, John (Uncle Reff); Page 16 Public Domain (2); Page 17 Guy Billet, BritishWarGraves.co.uk; Page 18 Nigel Stevens, CWGC; Page 19 CWGC (2); Page 20 BritishWarGraves.co.uk CWGC; Page 21 CWGC (2); Page 22 Archie Needs, BritishWarGraves.co.uk; Page 23 CWGC (2); Page 24 Geoffrey Gillan, Public Domain; Page 25 Church Crawler; Page 26 CWGC (2); Page 27 CWGC (2); Page 28 A Powell-Thomas (2); Page 29 Dirk Debleu CWGC (2); Page 30 Senthil Nathan (2); Page 31 CWGC (2); Page 32 Nigel Stevens; Page 33 Nigel Stevens, Tony Emptage; Page 34 Tony Emptage (2); Page 35 Dirk Debleu CWGC (2); Page 36 Nigel Stevens, CWGC; Page 37 Sam Mundell, Dirk Debleu; Page 38 CWGC, Nigel Stevens; Page 39 Robert O'Connor, A Powell-Thomas; Page 40 Simon Godley, BritishWarGraves.co.uk; Page 41 Duncan R2, Rene Hourdry; Page 42 British War Graves, Rene Hourdry; Page 43 Rene Hourdry, British War Graves; Page 44 Anais Pancrazy, Page 45 British War Graves (2); Page 46 British War Graves; Page 47 British War Graves (2); Page 48 CWGC, Lucie Balin; Page 49 Public Domain, Wernervc; Page 50 Archie Needs, British War Graves; Page 51 J Smitheon (2); Page 52 Emilie Le Ny, Peter Bennett; Page 53 Russ Davies, A Powell-Thomas; Page 54 CWGC, Bob the Greenacre cat; Page 55 CWGC (2); Page 56 Geert Brouckaert; Page 57 Sam Mundell (2); Page 58 Nigel Stevens; Page 59 Nigel Stevens; Page 60 Kevin Garcia; Page 61 Gary Dee; Page 62 Nigel Stevens; Page 63 Public Domain; Page 64 A Powell-Thomas; Page 65 Richard Dudley, public domain; Page 66 CWGC; Page 67 Silvarius Celso, Kart Shutter Arts; Page 68 Claude Laignel; Page 69 public domain (2); Page 70 British War Graves, public domain; Page 71 British War Graves, public domain; Page 72 C Fulbright; Page 73 Asia War Graves .com, Hagai Agmon-Snir; page 74 Bob the Greenacre Cat, Velvet; Page 75 VC & GC Association; Page 76 CWGC, A Powell-Thomas (2); Page 77 Tony Emptage; Page 78 Devon Church Crawler, A Powell-Thomas; Page 79 Havang, Devon Church Crawler; Page 80 CWGC, Uncle Reff; Page 81 CWGC, Uncle Reff; Page 82 Roland Unger; Page 83 Roland Unger, CWGC; Page 84 CWGC; Page 85 CWGC; Page 86 British War Graves; Page 87 AirWolfHound, British War Graves; Page 88 A Powell-Thomas (2); Page 89 CWGC (2); Page 90 djstanto, Tracey van Oeffelen, Nicola Quaceci; Page 91 CWGC; Page 92 Russ Davies, A Powell-Thomas; Page 93 CWGC (2); Page 94 CWGC, A Kipling; Page 95 Terence Ong, CWGC; Page 96 A Powell-Thomas (2); Page 97 A Powell-Thomas, CWGC; Page 98 A Powell-Thomas (3); Page 99 A Powell-Thomas (3); Back Cover A Powell-Thomas.

www.ingramcontent.com/pod-product-compliance
Lightning Source LLC
Chambersburg PA
CBHW042225090526
44584CB00001BA/15